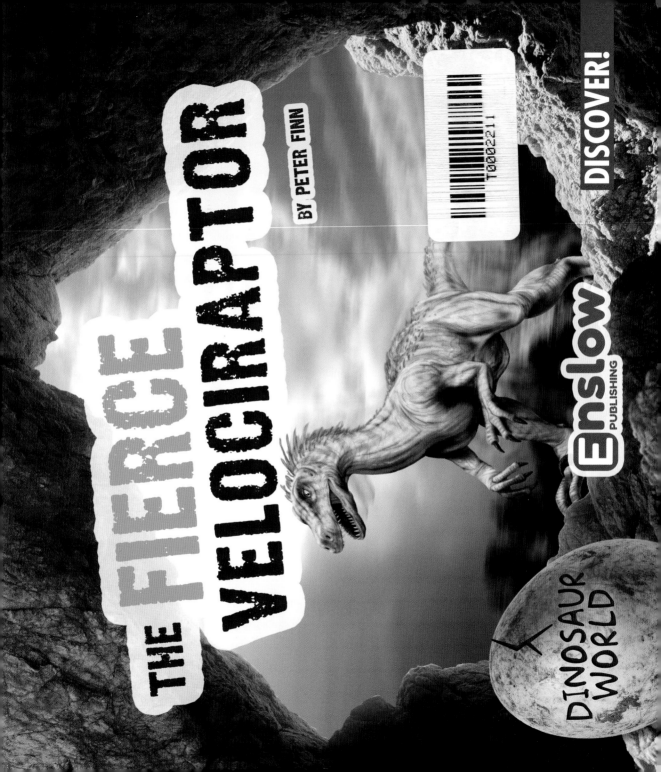

THE FIERCE VELOCIRAPTOR

BY PETER FINN

DISCOVER!

Enslow
PUBLISHING

DINOSAUR WORLD

Please visit our website, www.enslow.com. For a free color catalog of all our high-quality books, call toll free
1-800-398-2504 or fax 1-877-980-4454.

Library of Congress Cataloging-in-Publication Data

Names: Finn, Peter, 1978- author.
Title: The fierce velociraptor / Peter Finn.
Description: New York : Enslow Publishing, [2022] | Series: Dinosaur world
| Includes index.
Identifiers: LCCN 2020048535 (print) | LCCN 2020048536 (ebook) | ISBN
9781978521087 (library binding) | ISBN 9781978521063 (ebook) | ISBN
9781978521070 (set) | ISBN 9781978521094 (ebook)
Subjects: LCSH: Velociraptor—Juvenile literature.
Classification: LCC QE862.S3 F557 2022 (print) | LCC QE862.S3 (ebook) |
DDC 567.912-dc23
LC record available at https://lccn.loc.gov/2020048535
LC ebook record available at https://lccn.loc.gov/2020048536

Copyright © 2022 Enslow Publishing

Published in 2022 by
Enslow Publishing
101 West 23rd Street, Suite #240
New York, NY 10011

Designer: Sarah Liddell
Interior Layout: Rachel Rising
Editor: Therese Shea

Illustrations by Jeffrey Mangiat
Science Consultant: Philip J. Currie, Ph.D., Professor and Canada Research
Chair of Dinosaur Palaeobiology at the University of Alberta, Canada

Portions of this work were originally authored by Cory Lee and published as Velociraptor. All new material this edition authored
by Peter Finn.

Photo credits: Cover, pp. 1, 5, 7, 9, 11, 13, 15, 17, 19, 21 (rock border)SirinR/Shutterstock.com; pp. 2, 4, 6, 8, 10, 12, 14, 16, 18, 20,
22, 23, 24 (background) altanaka/Shutterstock.com; pp. 5, 7, 19 (egg) fotoslaz/Shutterstock.com.

Printed in the United States of America

CPSIA compliance information: Batch #CSENS22: For further informatio—n contact Enslow Publishing, New York, New York, at 1-800-398-2504.

Find us on [f] [o]

CONTENTS

Boldface words appear in Words to Know.

MEET VELOCIRAPTOR

Are the biggest dinosaurs the scariest dinosaurs? Meet Velociraptor. It wasn't big. However, it was **fierce**, fast, smart, and hungry! This dinosaur lived more than 70 **million** years ago. Velociraptor **fossils** can tell us a lot about it.

HOW TO SAY
VELOCIRAPTOR:
VUH-LAH-SUH-
RAP-TUHR

THE SPEEDY ROBBER

In 1923, scientists discovered the first Velociraptor fossil. They found a **skull** and a toe claw. They named this dinosaur Velociraptor. That means "speedy robber." They believed the name **described** how this meat-eating dinosaur acted.

SCIENTISTS THOUGHT VELOCIRAPTOR LOOKED LIKE A FAST DINOSAUR THAT STOLE EGGS AND OTHER FOOD. 7

NOT TOO TALL

Velociraptor was about as tall as a big dog. Most were no taller than 2 feet (61 cm). However, they could grow to be 6 feet (1.8 m) long. They had short arms and a big head. A long tail helped them **balance** when they ran.

2 FEET (61 CM) TALL

FEATHERS

Velociraptor had feathers on its body! A fossil proved this. Velociraptor was like a bird in other ways too. It had **hollow** bones. It also laid eggs in nests. However, Velociraptor's arms were too short to fly.

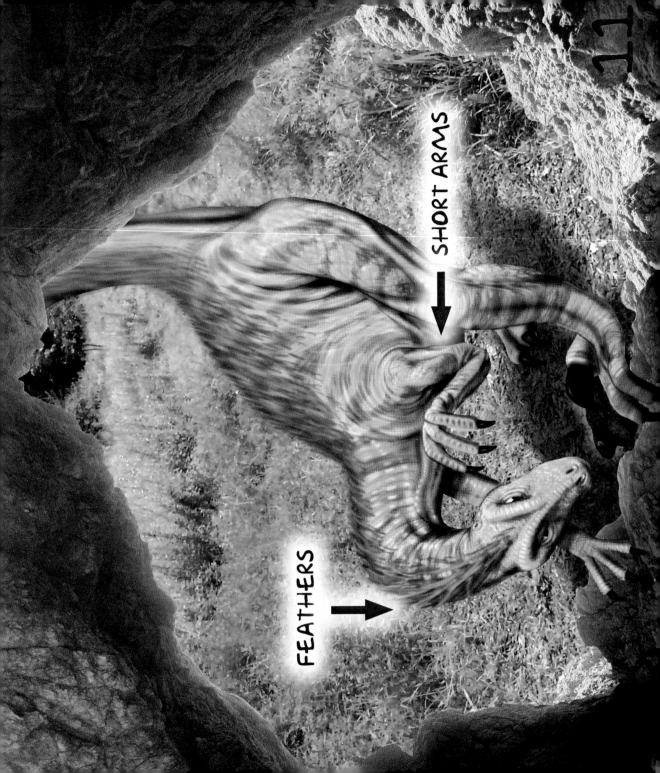

SHARP CLAWS

Each Velociraptor arm had three sharp claws. Velociraptor feet had claws too. Each foot had an extra long claw called a talon. The talon was for holding and kicking **prey**. The dinosaur walked with its talons up to keep them sharp!

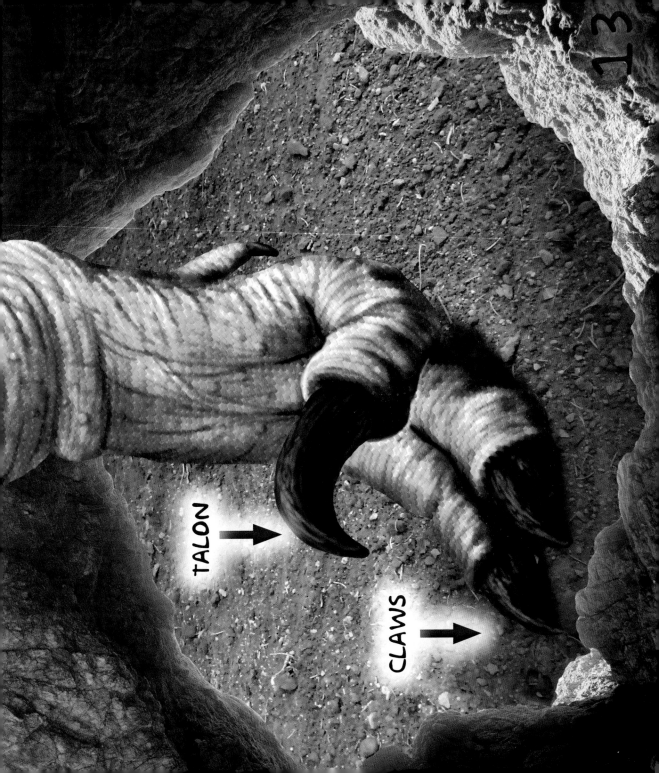

TALON →

CLAWS →

13

SMART AND FAST

Scientists think Velociraptor was smarter than many kinds of dinosaurs. It had a large brain for its body. It could run 25 miles (40 km) an hour too! Being smart and fast helped Velociraptor hunt its prey.

LARGE BRAIN

ITS PREY

Velociraptor hunted mostly smaller dinosaurs and other animals. One fossil found was a Velociraptor and a *Protoceratops* in the middle of a fight! They were both killed by something like a sandstorm. Velociraptor likely didn't hunt such a large dinosaur often.

VELOCIRAPTOR

PROTOCERATOPS

SCAVENGER

Velociraptor was a scavenger too. That means it ate dead animals that it found. Scientists found the bone of a large dinosaur inside a Velociraptor fossil. This likely means the Velociraptor found the dead or dying dinosaur.

VELOCIRAPTOR HAD UP TO 30 SHARP TEETH.

MORE TO FIND OUT

Scientists aren't sure if Velociraptor hunted in packs. They wonder if its feathers helped keep its nest warm. More Velociraptor fossils have been found in the Gobi Desert of Asia. These might help us find answers to Velociraptor questions!

VELOCIRAPTOR

FEATHERS

LARGE BRAIN

LONG TAIL

SIZE OF A
BIG DOG

TALONS ON
FEET

MEAT EATER

WORDS TO KNOW

balance Being able to stay in place without falling.

describe To say what something is like.

fierce Ready to kill or fight.

fossil The hardened marks or remains of plants and animals that formed over thousands or millions of years.

hollow Having nothing inside.

million A thousand thousands, or 1,000,000.

prey An animal that is hunted by other animals for food.

skull The bony frame of the head and face.

FOR MORE INFORMATION

BOOKS

Carr, Aaron. *Velociraptor.* New York, NY: AV2, 2021.

Radley, Gail. *Velociraptor.* Mankato, MN: Black Rabbit Books, 2021.

Ringstad, Arnold. *Velociraptor.* Minneapolis, MN: Cody Koala, 2019.

WEBSITES

Paleontology: The Big Dig
www.amnh.org/explore/ology/paleontology
Learn about the science of ancient life.

Velociraptor Facts for Kids
www.sciencekids.co.nz/sciencefacts/dinosaurs/velociraptor.html
Read some quick facts about this dinosaur.

Publisher's note to educators and parents: Our editors have carefully reviewed these websites to ensure that they are suitable for students. Many websites change frequently, however, and we cannot guarantee that a site's future contents will continue to meet our high standards of quality and educational value. Be advised that students should be closely supervised whenever they access the internet.

INDEX